Beautiful Together

Written & designed by Alexandra Fuller
Illustrated by Iryna Rohachova

Hi, my name is RED, what's your name?

My name is ORANGE!

Orange? Why aren't you red?

Hm, I don't know. But I look like a fruit and sound like one. And I love being orange. Why aren't you orange?

Hey,
we are red and
orange, what's
your name?

My name is YELLOW,

Interesting, so you are not red or orange, why are you YELLOW?

I'm not sure,
but I look like the sun.
And I love being yellow.
Why are you guys red
and orange?

Hi! We are RED, ORANGE, and YELLOW, what's your name?

My name is GREEN,

Really?
Why are you green
and not red,
or orange,
or yellow?

Well, I don't know, but I love being green and I look like the grass. Why aren't you green?

Oh hi,
we are red, orange,
yellow, and green,
what's your
name?

My name is BLUE!

Wow, blue...
You do not look like
any of us.
Why are you blue?

Well, I am not so sure, but I look like the sky, and the ocean, and I love being blue. Why aren't you blue?

Hello!
We are red, yellow,
orange, green, and blue.
What's your
name?

My name is INDIGO.

Indigo? Hm... Why aren't you like us?

I look like that house over there and that beautiful flower and I love my color. Why don't you look like me?

Oh hey!
We are red, orange, yellow, green, blue, and indigo.
What's your name?

My name is VIOLET!

Wow violet! You kind of look like indigo, but have your own shade... Hm!

Yeah,
that seems true,
but I don't look
like any of you,

Come closer and let's see what we look like TOGETHER!

Wouldn't you know?

Even though we are all different, when we stand together...

We make one beautiful rainbow!